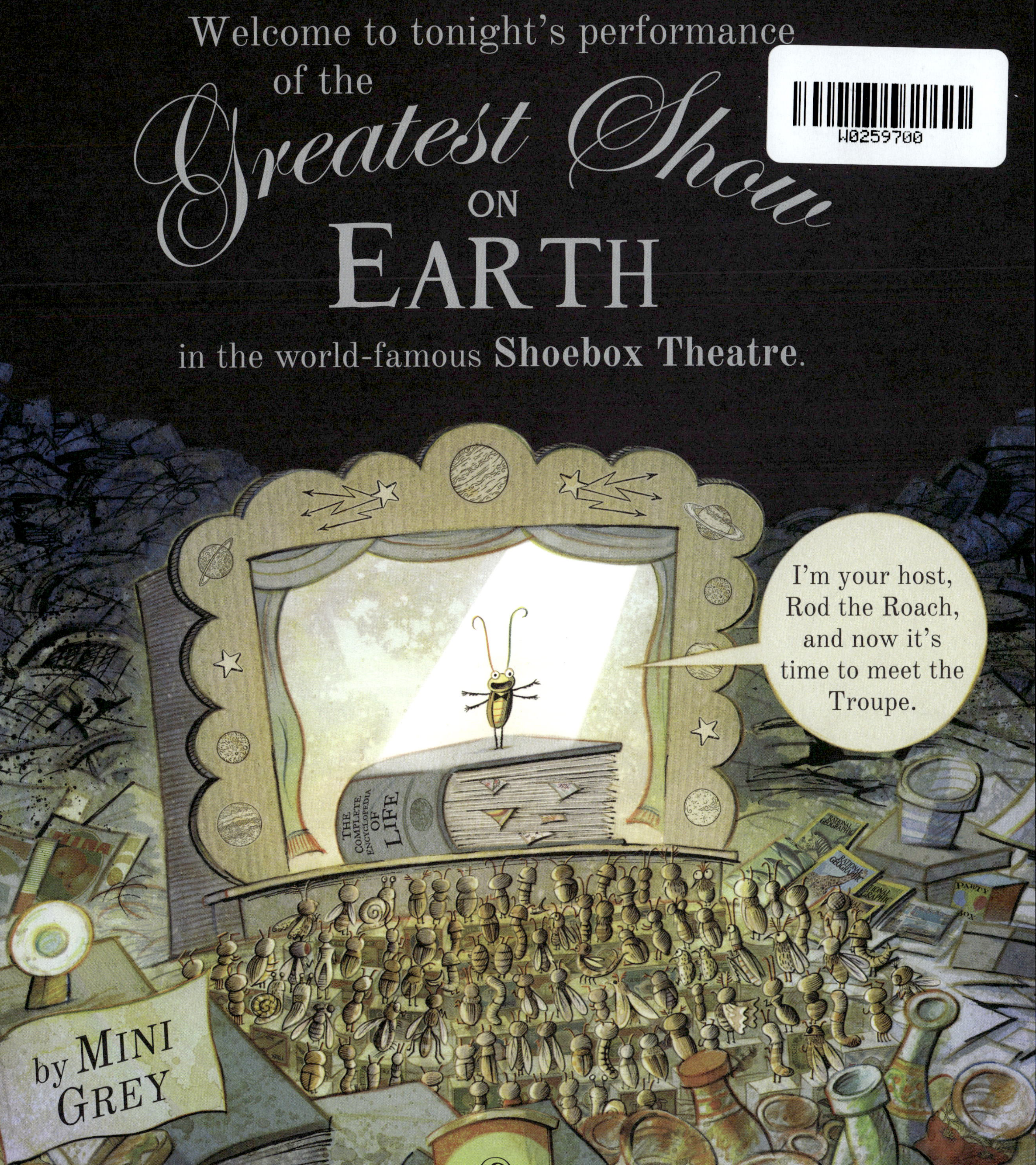
Welcome to tonight's performance
of the
Greatest Show
ON
EARTH
in the world-famous Shoebox Theatre.
I'm your host,
Rod the Roach,
and now it's
time to meet the
Troupe.
THE COMPLETE ENCYCLOPEDIA OF LIFE
by MINI
GREY
PUFFIN

PLAN OF THE SHOE
Here are THE WINGS, where we have a closer look at the story . . .
(. . . with Annika Ant.)
Here's the MAIN STAGE, where the Troupe act out the story of Life on Earth.
(Read this bit first.)
Your performers tonight are Pierre, Cedric, Gary, Malia, Alonzo, Brunhilda and Edna.
Say hello, Troupe!
THE COMPLETE ENCYCLOPEDIA OF LIFE
4.6
billion years

Down here is the Orchestra Pit,
where we have the team in charge of the Tape Measure of Time:
Anton, Anatole and Annette. *Say hello, Time Team!*

INGREDIENTS
for your
Earth-like Planet
You will need:
Carbon
(We made this carbon by burning some toast.)
Oxygen
(Watch out – it's flammable!)
O
Iron
(This has got a bit rusty.)
Magnesium
(Nearly took my feelers off!)
Silica
(This is Silicon Dioxide, AKA sand.)
Calcium
(Shells, bones and teeth are built of calcium.)
A pinch of Sulphur
(Whoooo, that's eggy!)
and plenty of ice.
It's 4.6 Billion
Mr Doughball
INSTAPUFF
4.6
billion years
4590 MYA
4591 MYA
4592 MYA
4593 MYA
4594 MYA

Years Ago . . .

This is it,
ladies and gentlemen.
As we **raise**
the curtain . . .

THE STORY OF LIFE

is about to begin!

It's time to
COOK UP
an Earth-like planet.

HOW TO COOK UP AN EARTH-LIKE PLANET

Take your ingredients and mix them up at high speed in your Cosmic Blender until they're really hot and start to form a lump of molten mixture.

Place the lump at the right distance from a young star so it is not too hot or too cold. It will be quite steamy.

Leave it for a few hundred million years to cool. Watch as a golden-brown crust forms and the steam settles down . . .

and condenses into a lovely watery ocean.

1 ← Every centimetre on the Tape Measure of Time stands for **ONE MILLION YEARS**

HOW TO KEEP YOUR NEW WORLD SAFE

You'll need well-behaved NEIGHBOUR PLANETS

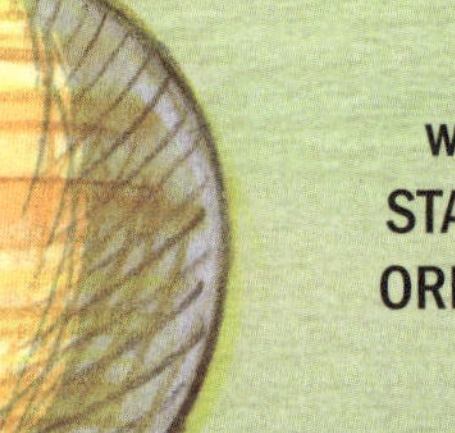

with STABLE ORBITS.

You'll need a MOON to stabilize your orbit and rotation,

and a MAGNETIC FIELD

to protect you from the Solar Wind,

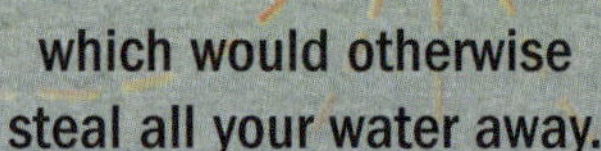

which would otherwise steal all your water away.

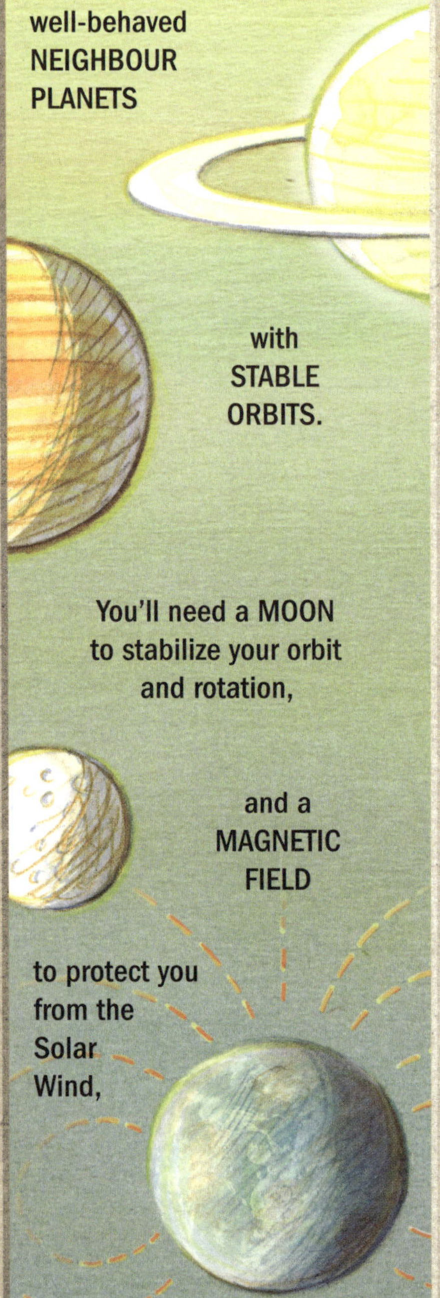

It's 4.6 Billion

Here is the young Earth.

It has only just been built.

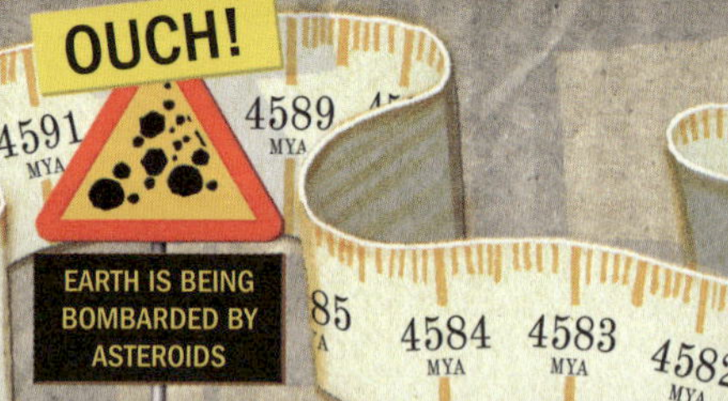

Years Ago
It is hot and bothered and bursting with lava.
HOW TO KEEP YOUR NEW WORLD SAFE
You also need to be the right distance from the Sun.
If you're too close,
YOU GET VENUS – too hot!
If you're too far away, you get MARS – too cold.
SPARKLERS 3
VESUVIUS
MATCHES
YOW! COLLISION WITH MYSTERY PLANET, 'THEIA'
THE MOON IS BORN
4575 MYA
4570 MYA
4569 MYA
4565 MYA
4564 MYA
4559 MYA
4558 MYA
4552 MYA

The World of MICROBES

Let's go back to 3.8 billion years ago. Earth is less than a billion years old, but something like life has already got started.

Earth is coated with an ocean of shallow, salty seas (there's hardly any dry land at all), and it's in these seas that life happened.

Molecules have arisen that can COPY themselves. Maybe they are near a hot volcanic vent where there are lots of minerals they can use.

The molecules make themselves a jacket to live in – and now they're single-celled microbes.

Years Ago . . .
It might have looked like not much was going on, but LIFE has got started.
Welcome to the WORLD OF MICROBES.
(And *Hi!* to all you microbes in the audience.)
The World of
MICROBES
Some microbes build into clumps and mats and mounds.
These may look like big old rocks to you, but they're
LIFE FORMS
made of colonies of microbes!
They're stromatolites.
Howdy, Stromies!
The Stromies build up in layers over years and years. New microbes (they're blue-green algae) grow on the top layer, using energy from the Sun. Slowly, slowly, they breathe out
OXYGEN,
changing the air of the planet.
3 BILLION YEARS AGO
EARTH'S ATMOSPHERE IS MOSTLY CARBON DIOXIDE
THOSE BLUE-GREEN ALGAE JUST KEEP BURPING OUT OXYGEN
OXYGENOMETER
OXYGEN LEVELS ARE RISING IN THE SEA
2992 MYA
2989 MYA
2988 MYA
2987 MYA

JOURNEY TO THE CENTRE OF THE EARTH

Let's slice Earth open and have a look inside this delicious pudding of a planet.

A DRIZZLE OF OCEAN
CRISPY CRUSTY LAYERS
THICK CONTINENTAL CRUST
THIN OCEAN CRUST
WARM MELTY MANTLE (constantly swirling with currents)
HOT LIQUID METAL OUTER CORE
EVEN HOTTER CRYSTALIZED IRON INNER CORE

Here's a MANTLE PLUME making a HOT SPOT . . . Watch out for a LAVA BREAKOUT!

2.5 BILLION

The Rise of the Continents

BEST BEFORE FEB/2040 1233

BLUE-GREEN ALGAE ARE ON THE RISE

THOSE BLUE-GREEN ALGAE KEEP ON BUBBLING OUT OXYGEN

NOW OXYGEN IS INCREASING IN EARTH'S ATMOSPHERE, CHANGING THE AIR OF THE PLANET

2547 MYA 2546 MYA 2545 MYA 2517 MYA 2516 MYA 2515 MYA 2514 MYA 2513 MYA 2512 MYA 2511 MYA

Years Ago
Earth has been a water world so far, but now it has cooled down enough for thick crusts to be pushed up out of the seas.
(Things were too hot and molten before now – new land made by lava from volcanoes just sank back in.)
They're the first continents.
LET'S LOOK AT WHAT'S HAPPENING UNDER THE SEA
Here's a big rift on a hot spot where lava is bubbling up, making new ocean crust and pushing these continents apart.
PUSH
PUSH
PUSH
PUSH
PUSH
New Crust Forming
PULL
PULL
PULL
Here's a rip where crust is being pulled under.
This is the slow PUSH and PULL of the continents around the planet.
2.5 BILLION YEARS AGO
2491 MYA
2490 MYA
2489 MYA
2488 MYA
OXYGENOMETER
OXYGEN LEVELS ARE RISING IN THE AIR
2484 MYA
2483 MYA
2482 MYA
EARTH IS COOLING DOWN
2468 MYA
WATCH OUT! THERE'S GOING TO BE A FREEZE.
2465 MYA
2464 MYA
ICEHOUSE MASS EXTINCTION COMING UP

Around 600

LIFE WITH THE EDIACARANS

It's 600 million years ago, and oxygen levels in the air and sea have been slowly growing . . .

(thank you, Stromies!)

...but deep down here in the oceans, life has got **interesting**.

Look at them – cells have grouped together to make **bodies**.

Life is relaxed down here with the Ediacarans.

It's now less than one billion years ago and life is getting clumpier.

Welcome to the Age of Jelly.

Everyone is quite squidgy and eyes haven't been invented yet.

Million Years Ago
LIFE WITH THE EDIACARANS
They are all sorts of bogglingly odd shapes.
Some have stalks to hold on to the bottom.
Some are like leaves and discs. And some are very like sponges and jellyfish and anemones.
They have no eyes
or legs
or heads,
or mouths,
but they're the first things we can call **animals**.
These folks mostly wave about gently and feed on nutrients that drift by.
PANNOTIA SUPERCONTINENT IS GROUPED AROUND THE SOUTH POLE
600 MILLION YEARS AGO
EARTH IS WARMING UP
CHARNIA
CLOUDINA
MEDUSA
KIMBERELLA
BRACHIDIUM
DICKINSONIA
SPRIGGINA
BIOTA
594 MYA
589
585 MYA
584 MYA
583 MYA

It's around 500 million years ago. Earth is still mostly under water, and in the water is where it's all happening.

Come in, have a look, because life has REALLY speeded up. Maybe it's because of these EYES!

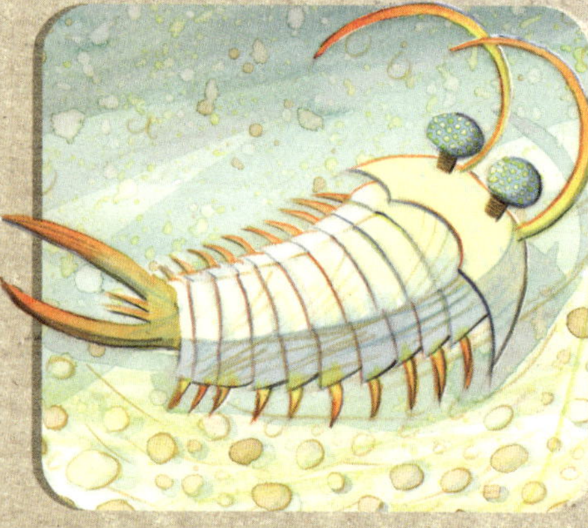

This little chap is a **Trilobite**, and has maybe the first eyes with lenses – made of **CRYSTAL!**

541 Million

That must have been the Cambrian Explosion!

It's an EXPLOSION of new life forms.

Look at all these new inventions!

Which way up does this thing go?

Don't ask me!

571 MYA 570 MYA 563 MYA 558 MYA 555 MYA

Years Ago (precisely)
Did you hear a BANG?
They've got EYES.
They've got LEGS.
They can go fast.
They can be PREDATORS.
Animals have invented having a FEEDING HOLE, and if you have one of those, then you need an EXCRETION HOLE at the other end.
Fig. A
Fig. B
Fig. C
Fig. D
Fig. E
SCRAM!
If you've got EYES, you'd want them near your Feeding Hole (not down the Bum End) – so we get a Front and a Back!
UP
BACK
LEFT
RIGHT
FRONT
DOWN
With eyes and a feeding hole, you can start searching for lunch; you'd better start MOVING – so we get an up-side and a down-side and a left-side and a right-side – and these inventions stick around for ever after.
ICE AT
POLES
543 MYA
541 MILLION YEARS AGO
WELCOME TO THE CAMBRIAN. HAVE A NICE DAY.
IT'S A WARM GREENHOUSE WORLD
ANOMALOCARIS
HALLUCIGENIA
MARRELLA
533 MYA
OPABINIA
ANIMAL LIFE SURGES!
TRILOBITE
526 MYA
525 MYA

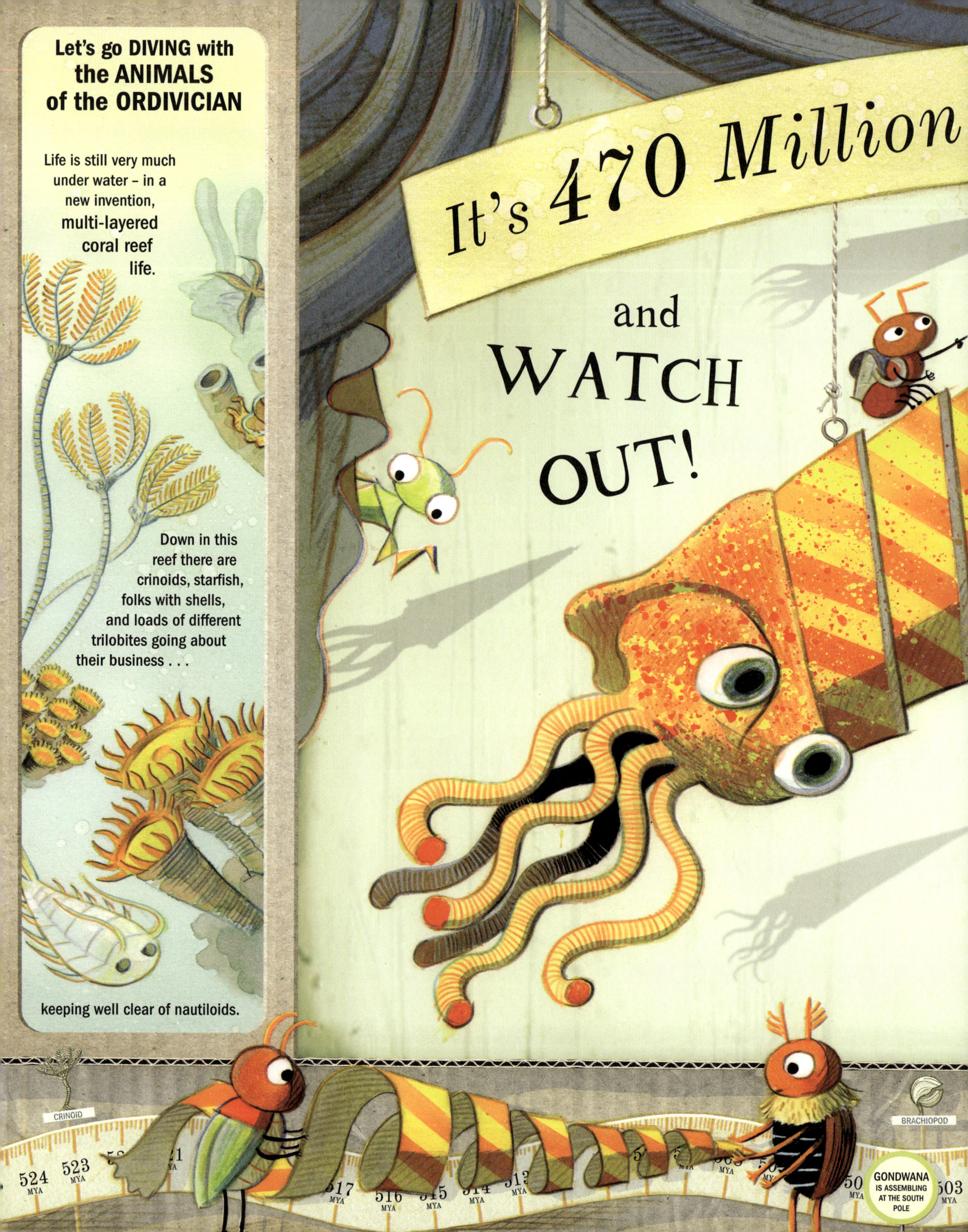
Let's go DIVING with the ANIMALS of the ORDIVICIAN
Life is still very much under water – in a new invention, multi-layered coral reef life.
Down in this reef there are crinoids, starfish, folks with shells, and loads of different trilobites going about their business . . .
keeping well clear of nautiloids.
It's 470 Million
and WATCH OUT!
CRINOID
BRACHIOPOD
524 MYA
523 MYA
516 MYA
503 MYA
GONDWANA IS ASSEMBLING AT THE SOUTH POLE

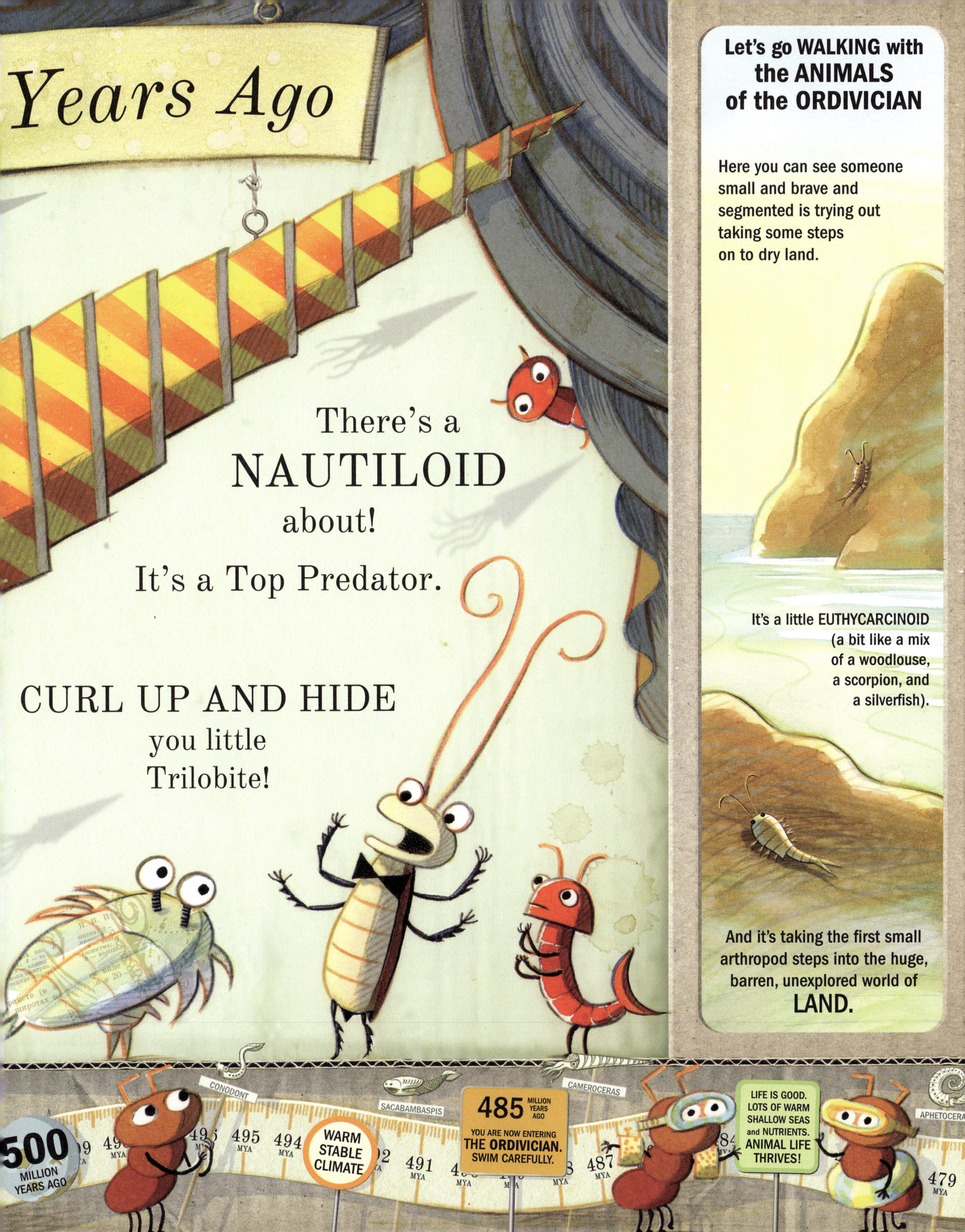

Years Ago
There's a NAUTILOID about!
It's a Top Predator.
CURL UP AND HIDE you little Trilobite!
Let's go WALKING with the ANIMALS of the ORDIVICIAN
Here you can see someone small and brave and segmented is trying out taking some steps on to dry land.
It's a little EUTHYCARCINOID (a bit like a mix of a woodlouse, a scorpion, and a silverfish).
And it's taking the first small arthropod steps into the huge, barren, unexplored world of LAND.
500 MILLION YEARS AGO
CONODONT
495 MYA
494 MYA
WARM STABLE CLIMATE
491 MYA
SACABAMBASPIS
485 MILLION YEARS AGO
YOU ARE NOW ENTERING THE ORDIVICIAN. SWIM CAREFULLY.
CAMEROCERAS
487 MYA
LIFE IS GOOD. LOTS OF WARM SHALLOW SEAS and NUTRIENTS. ANIMAL LIFE THRIVES!
APHETOCERAS
479 MYA

Just look at these
JAWLESS BEAUTIES
swimming in the shallow seas of the Silurian . . .
These fish did have mouths – but no jaws, so they could only eat small food.
But maybe there's a way of getting your teeth into something
BIGGER . . .
THE AGE OF
457 MYA
450 MILLION YEARS AGO
PROTOTAXITES
THE PLANET IS COOLING
ICEHOUSE
MASS EXTINCTION
444 MYA
443 MYA
443 MILLION YEARS AGO
WELCOME TO THE SILURIAN. PLEASE PLAY NICELY.
ONYCHOPHORA
442 MYA
441 MYA
440 MYA

FISH
BEGAN 420 MILLION YEARS AGO
OPEN WIDE!
It's the invention of JAWS.
Now these critters can take a proper BITE out of you!
Acanthodian spiny fish,
Placoderm armoured fish,
the first sharks,
bony fish with lobe fins.
And this LOBE FIN is going to come in HANDY in the future . . .
Here we are deep in the AGE of FISH.
This big old chap is a DUNKLEOSTEUS, a bony armoured monster placoderm.
Watch out, you little spiny-finned fish!
COOKSONIA
CEPHALASPIS
434 MYA
420 MYA
EARTH IS WARMING, ICE CAPS MELTING
WE HAVE A GREENHOUSE PLANET: NO ICE AND WARM, SHALLOW SEAS

PLANET PLANT
It's mid-afternoon in the Late Devonian.
One day, these plants will become the coal that humans just love to dig out of the ground.
Plants explore
Up till now most life has been in the seas, but now plant life is creeping over the rocky surface of Earth.
GEMUENDINA
421 MYA
420 MYA
419 MYA
418 MYA
419 MILLION YEARS AGO
YOU HAVE ARRIVED AT THE DEVONIAN.
415 MYA
SCORPION
PTERASPIS
408 MYA
EARTH IS VERY WARM; CO_2 LEVELS HIGH
SPIDER
403
400 MILLION YEARS AGO

the Land
400 Million Years Ago
PLANET PLANT
Blue-green algae had invented
PHOTOSYNTHESIS
ages ago, using carbon dioxide and the Sun's energy to build more body (out of the carbon) and release
OXYGEN.
(Remember those Stromatolites? That's what they were doing, 3 billion years ago.)
Plant cells use this invention too, in their own innovation: the LEAF.
Plants are changing the planet.
They are releasing oxygen into the atmosphere.
Their fallen leaves mulch down to make organic goodness in the soils.
Their roots hold those early soils together.
They are transforming Earth from a world of brown and blue . . .
into a planet of GREEN and blue.
PLANTS GET TALL
396 MYA
395 MYA
AMMONITE
FORESTS COVER THE LAND
390 MYA
ACANTHODIAN
EUSTHENOPTERON
384 MYA
LIFE IS LUSH
(LOTS OF LOVELY PLANTS TO EAT)
DUNKLEOSTEUS
381 MYA
TIKTAALIK
377 MYA
376 MYA
375 MYA

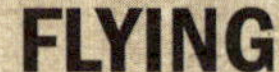

FLYING
has been a really popular invention on Earth, and yes,
US INSECTS
got there first!

Here's a Meganeura swooping about the swampy forests of the Carboniferous, with a whopping 72cm wingspan.

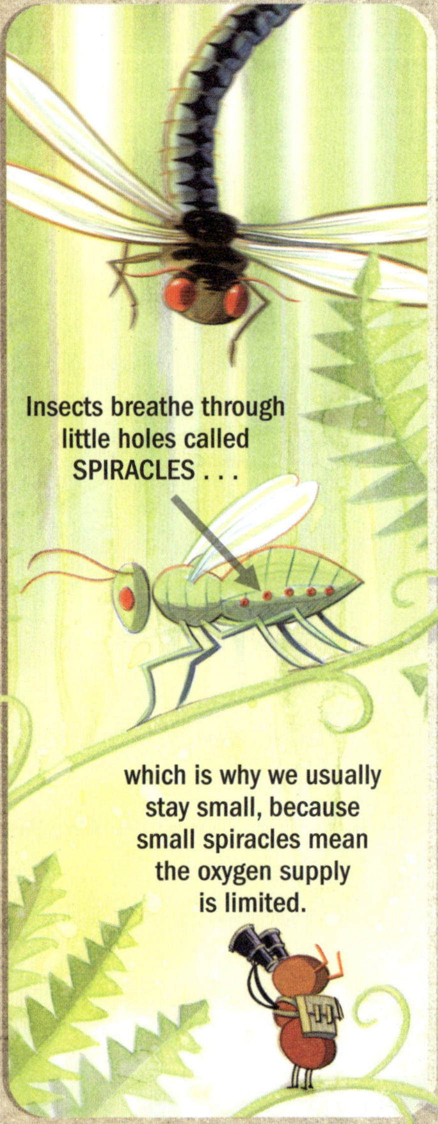

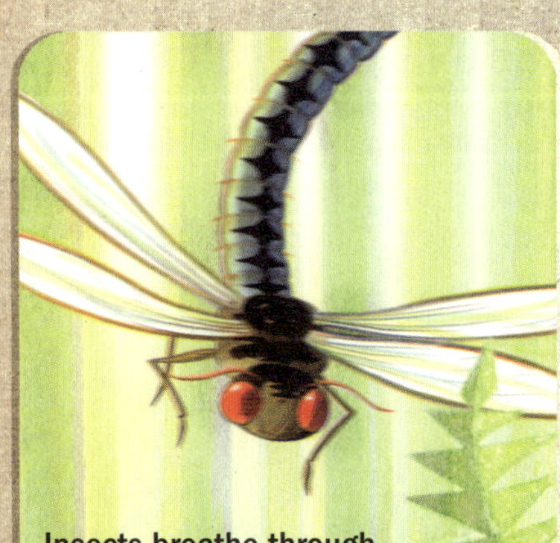

Insects breathe through little holes called SPIRACLES . . .

which is why we usually stay small, because small spiracles mean the oxygen supply is limited.

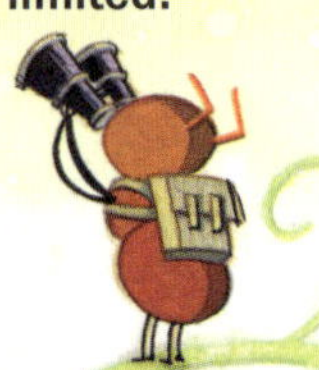

But if there's LOADS of Oxygen around, those spiracles can power a bigger insect body and we can have the most enormous insects ever seen . . .
so far . . .

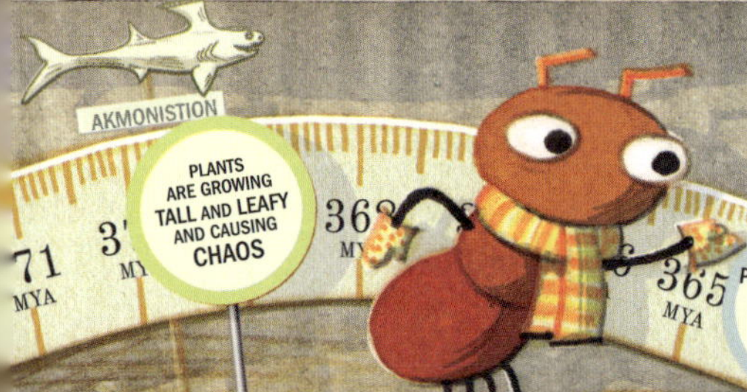

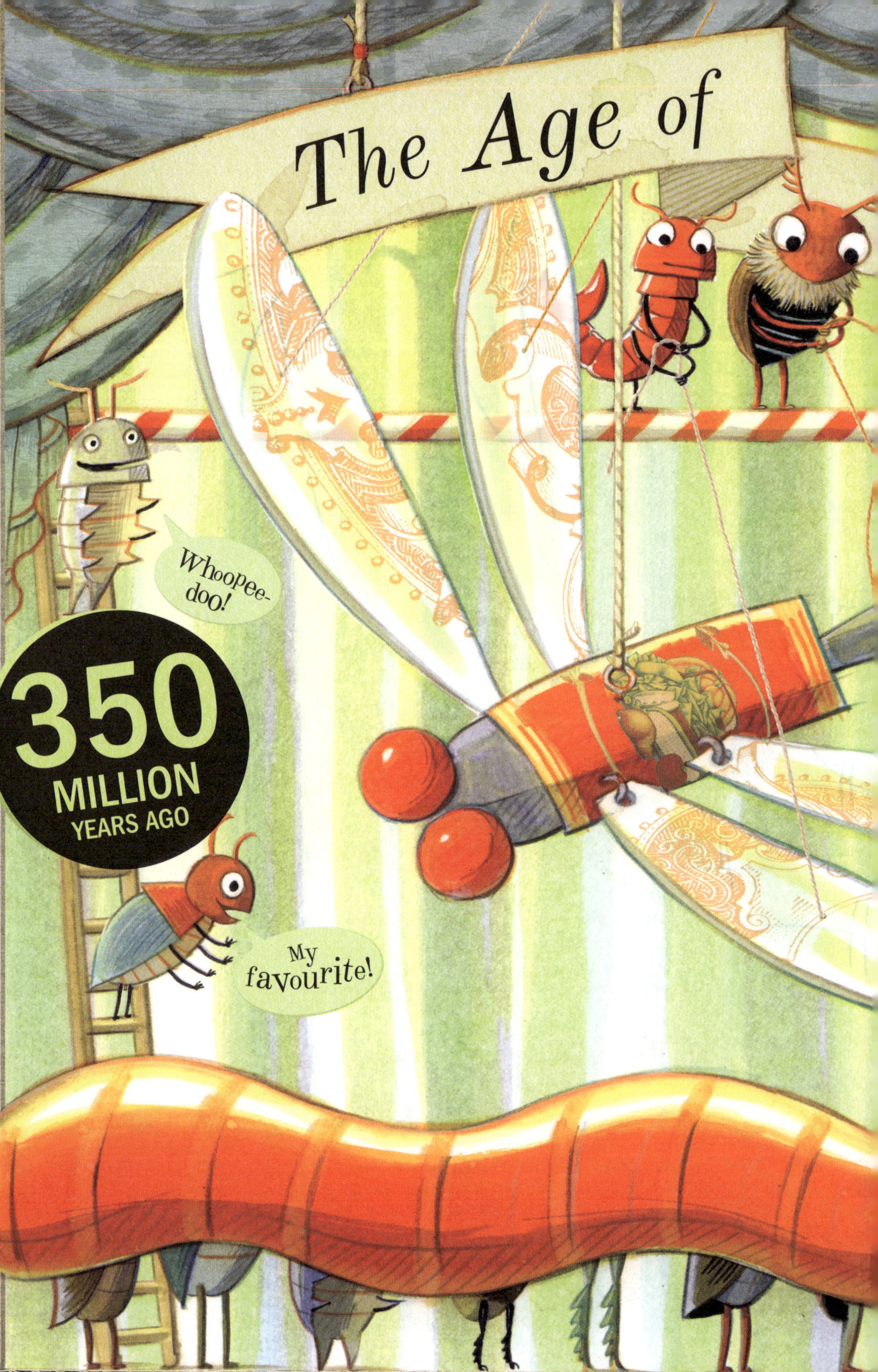
The Age of
Whoopee-doo!
350 MILLION YEARS AGO
My favourite!

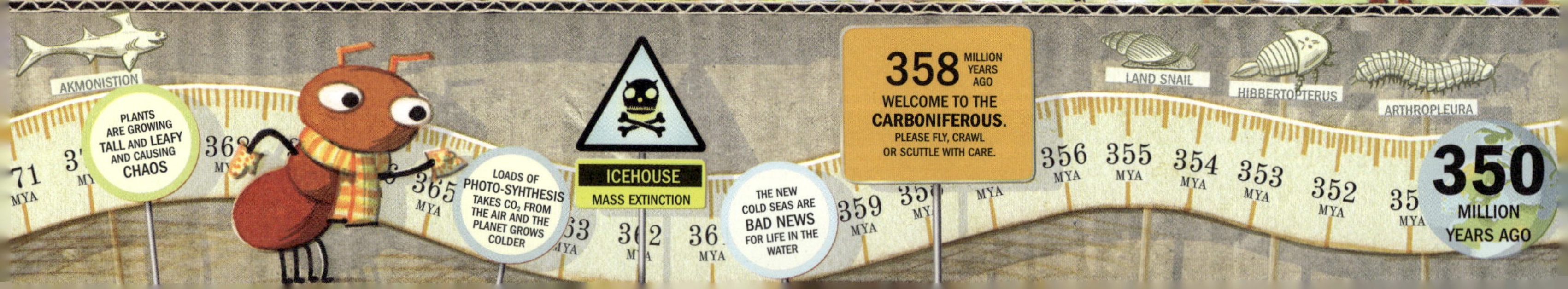
AKMONISTION
PLANTS ARE GROWING TALL AND LEAFY AND CAUSING CHAOS
365 MYA
LOADS OF PHOTO-SYHTHESIS TAKES CO2 FROM THE AIR AND THE PLANET GROWS COLDER
ICEHOUSE
MASS EXTINCTION
THE NEW COLD SEAS ARE BAD NEWS FOR LIFE IN THE WATER
359 MYA
358 MILLION YEARS AGO
WELCOME TO THE CARBONIFEROUS.
PLEASE FLY, CRAWL OR SCUTTLE WITH CARE.
356 MYA
355 MYA
354 MYA
353 MYA
352 MYA
LAND SNAIL
HIBBERTOPTERUS
ARTHROPLEURA
350 MILLION YEARS AGO

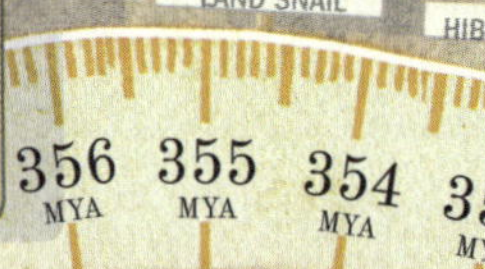

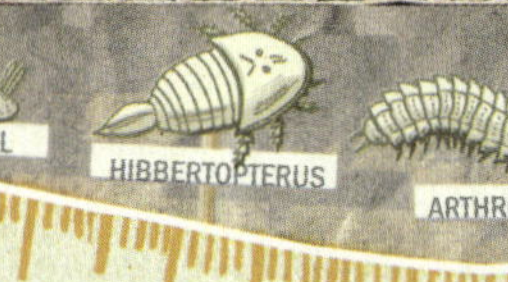

MASSIVE Insects
Now there's so much tasty plant life on land, animals are exploring out of the oceans.
Look – it's the first flying creatures.
Us insects have got really big.
ALL ABOUT oxygen
Now it's time to talk about that most reactive of the elements, OXYGEN, and how it makes things BURN.
OLD BOILER MATCHES
Our bodies use oxygen to burn food and make us GO. Oxygen is part of Earth's atmosphere (about 20% of the air nowadays). But in the past, that amount has changed. In Carboniferous times, oxygen levels got really high.
And WHY?
WHO was increasing the oxygen?
I'll tell you who: those FIRST PLANTS.
WE ARE OFFICIALLY IN THE AGE OF ARTHROPODS
347 MYA
346 MYA
345 MYA
COCKROACH
340 MYA
339 MYA
ACANTHOSTEGA
PEDERPES
ICHTHYOSTEGA
334 MYA
OXYGENOMETER
OXYGEN AT 20%
OXYGENOMETER
OXYGEN AT AN ALL-TIME HIGH: 35%!
MEGANEURA
327 MYA
326 MYA
325 MYA

PLANET of the NEWTS
Remember those lobe fins? Watch as gradually fins turn to legs in the long journey from FISH to POD.
Now, for the first time, animals with bones inside can wander about on dry land. They are the AMPHIBIANS.
Age of Amphibians
Extinct Amphibians
Fig. 12
FISH-O-POD
Extinct Amphibians
Fig. 43
NEWT-O-POD
TETRAPOD
EYES: TWO
ONE BODY
TAIL: OPTIONAL
325 MYA
324 MYA
GREAT FORESTS AND GIANT SWAMPS
317 MYA
BURIED PLANTS LOCK UP CARBON DIOXIDE . . .
314 MYA
. . . MAKING A COOLER PLANET, WITH ICE CAPS AT THE POLES
310 MYA
AMPHIBAMUS
DIPLOCAULUS
318 MILLION YEARS AGO
AMPHIBIANS RULE ON LAND
304 MYA

PLAN
ONE HEAD
FIVE DIGITS
LIMBS: FOUR
Extinct Amphibians Fig. 23
SPADE-O-POD
Extinct Amphibians Fig. 1
CUTE-O-POD
It's really about time to introduce the invention of the very popular TETRAPOD STYLE OF BODY.
PLANET of the NEWTS
Look at these Amphibian Inventions:
Arms and Legs!
Wrists!
Neck!
Fingers!
Elbows!
Hips!
Lungs!
Knees!
Toes!
But the amphibians still had to stay near water – their eggs couldn't live anywhere else.
298 MILLION YEARS AGO
YOU ARE ENTERING THE PERMIAN AGE
ERYOPS
COCKROACH
COCKROACHES RULE!
NEARLY 90% OF INSECTS ON LAND ARE SOME TYPE OF ROACH.
DIMETRODON
PELYCOSAURS RULE!
THEY MAKE UP 70% OF LAND VERTEBRATES
EDAPHOSAURUS
OPHIACODON
THE CONTINENTS OF GONDWANA AND LAURASIA ARE MOVING CLOSER
300 MILLION YEARS AGO
297 MYA
294 MYA
291 MYA
290 MYA
287 MYA
283 MYA
282 MYA

The DISASTER

Let's look at the state of Planet Earth 252 million years ago for some clues to why it all got so bad for life.

The land is nearly all joined together into one huge continent that stretches from pole to pole.

MASSIVE LAVA ERUPTIONS

PANGAEA

To make matters disastrous, giant lava flows belch out loads of carbon dioxide, and this blanket of gas makes the world get hotter and hotter.

So WHO was living in this terrible place?

DICYNODONT
MOSCHOPS
SCUTOSAURUS
GORGONOPS
PLACERIAS
EARTH'S CONTINENTS HAVE COME TOGETHER TO FORM PANGAEA
271 MYA 270 MYA 262 MYA 261 MYA 260 MYA
DANGER!
HAZARDS AHEAD!
252 MILLION YEARS AGO
WELCOME TO THE TRIASSIC
FASTEN YOUR SAFETY BELT!
LYSTROSAURUS
HOTHOUSE MASS EXTINCTION
250 MILLION YEARS AGO

Million
Years Ago
Grunt
PERMIAN MASS EXTINCTION is about to unfold.
The climate becomes extreme on land and sea.
Nearly everything dies.
But not quite . . .
The
SURVIVORS
Here we are in the very early Triassic, and who's here? Lystrosaurus, that's who. Nearly everyone is a lystrosaurus.
Maybe they were good at breathing the oxygen-poor air. Maybe they were good burrowers.
Maybe they just weren't fussy. But they were THE SURVIVORS.
But not quite the ONLY survivors . . .
I'm still alive!
(PROTO-DINO)
Me too!
(PROTO-MAMMAL)
VAST LAVA FLOWS
INTENSELY HIGH TEMPERATURES ON EARTH
LOW OXYGEN – IT'S HARD TO BREATHE
246 MYA
245 MYA
244 MYA
240
238
THRINAXODON
ASILISAURUS
CYNOGNATHUS
EUPARKERIA
PANGAEA STARTS TO BE PULLED APART LIKE A GIANT PIZZA
235 MYA
231 MYA
230 MYA
POSTOSUCHUS
NOTHOSAURUS
228 MYA
227 MYA
226 MYA

RISE OF THE

The **EGG** has changed everything.

Rather than laying an egg in a pond, this reptile has invented how to put a pond in an egg.

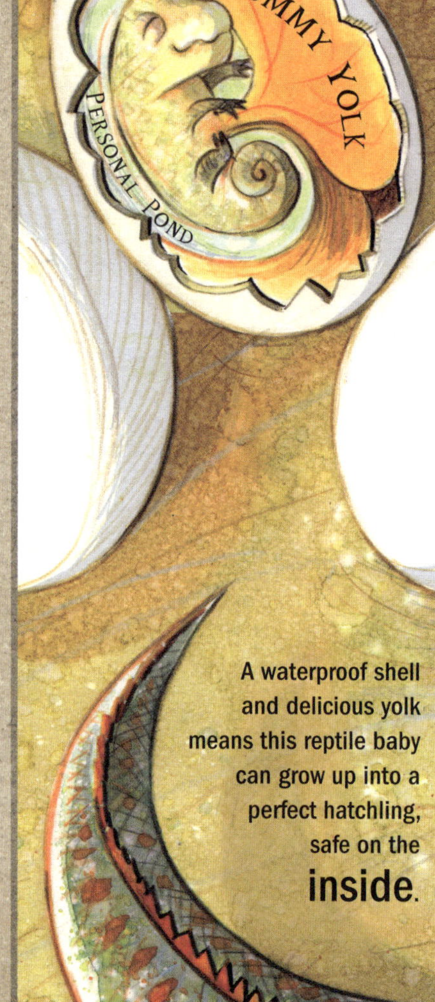

A waterproof shell and delicious yolk means this reptile baby can grow up into a perfect hatchling, safe on the **inside**.

SMILOSUCHUS,
A CROCODILE-LIKE PHYTOSAUR

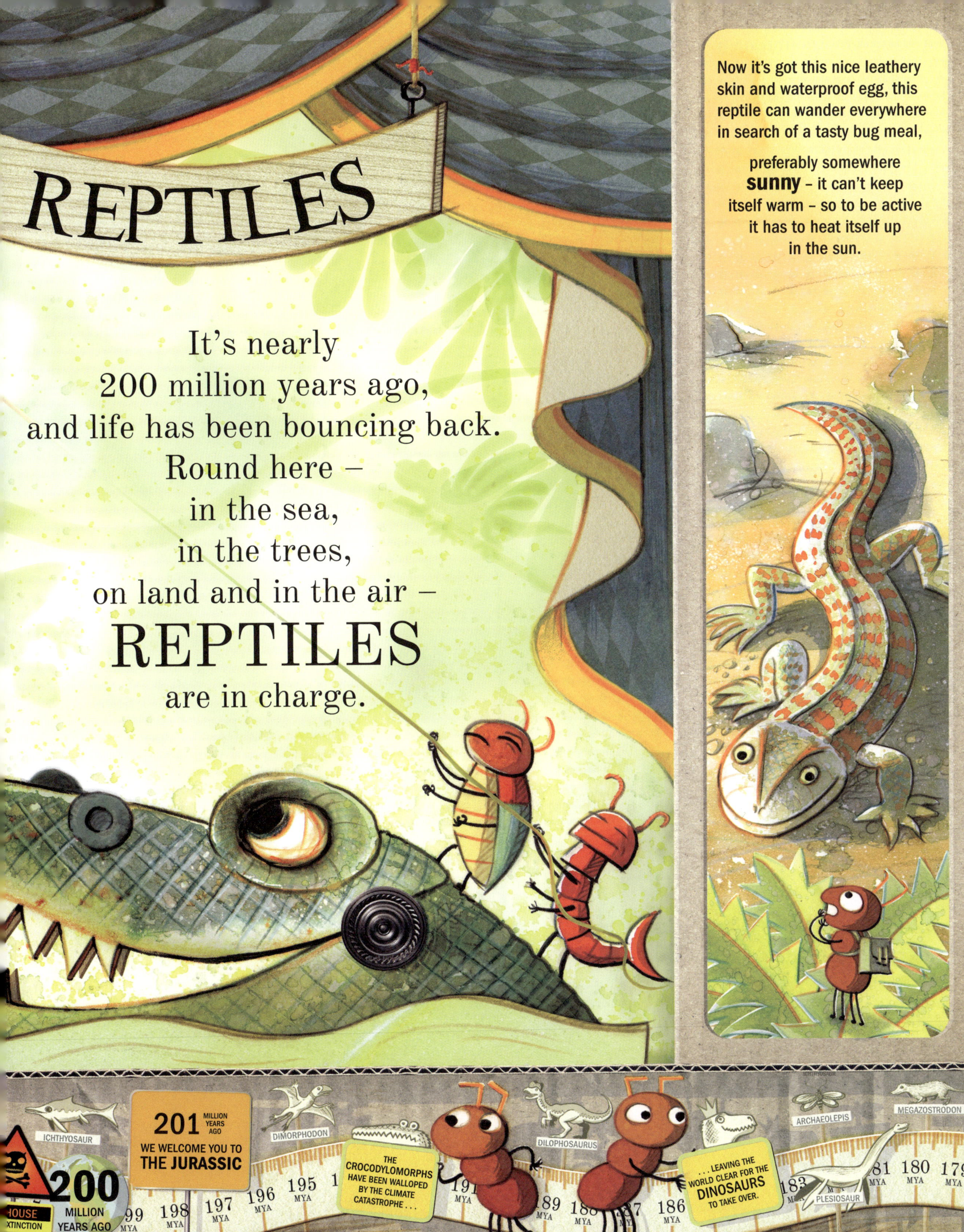
REPTILES
It's nearly
200 million years ago,
and life has been bouncing back.
Round here –
in the sea,
in the trees,
on land and in the air –
REPTILES
are in charge.
Now it's got this nice leathery skin and waterproof egg, this reptile can wander everywhere in search of a tasty bug meal,
preferably somewhere **sunny** – it can't keep itself warm – so to be active it has to heat itself up in the sun.
ICHTHYOSAUR
201 MILLION YEARS AGO
WE WELCOME YOU TO THE JURASSIC
DIMORPHODON
THE CROCODYLOMORPHS HAVE BEEN WALLOPED BY THE CLIMATE CATASTROPHE . . .
DILOPHOSAURUS
. . . LEAVING THE WORLD CLEAR FOR THE DINOSAURS TO TAKE OVER.
ARCHAEOLEPIS
MEGAZOSTRODON
PLESIOSAUR
200 MILLION YEARS AGO
198 MYA
197 MYA
196 MYA
195 MYA
186 MYA
180 MYA
179 MYA

PLANET OF THE GIANTS
Let's look down on mid-morning in the Jurassic as this Sauropod Posse comes swooping past.
Life has got really big.
Jurassic
150 MILLION YEARS AGO
Heave!
Nnng!
BELEMNITE
LIOPLEURODON
AMMONITE
ALLOSAURUS
ARCHAEOPTERYX
175 MILLION YEARS AGO
150 MILLION YEARS AGO
WARM GREENHOUSE CLIMATE

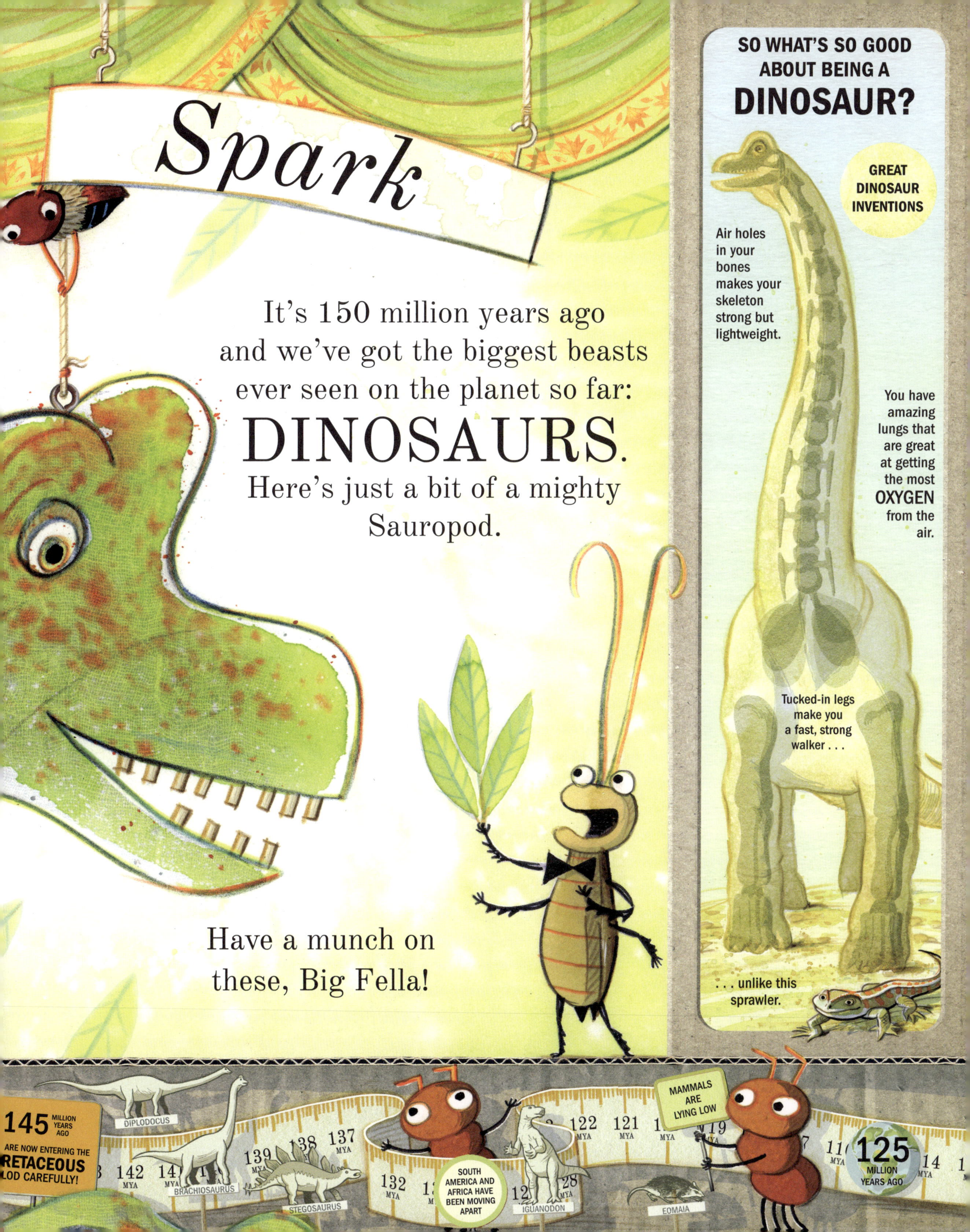
Spark
It's 150 million years ago
and we've got the biggest beasts
ever seen on the planet so far:
DINOSAURS.
Here's just a bit of a mighty
Sauropod.
Have a munch on
these, Big Fella!
SO WHAT'S SO GOOD
ABOUT BEING A
DINOSAUR?
GREAT
DINOSAUR
INVENTIONS
Air holes
in your
bones
makes your
skeleton
strong but
lightweight.
You have
amazing
lungs that
are great
at getting
the most
OXYGEN
from the
air.
Tucked-in legs
make you
a fast, strong
walker . . .
. . . unlike this
sprawler.
145 MILLION YEARS AGO
ARE NOW ENTERING THE
RETACEOUS
LOD CAREFULLY!
DIPLODOCUS
BRACHIOSAURUS
STEGOSAURUS
142 MYA
139 MYA
137 MYA
132 MYA
SOUTH
AMERICA AND
AFRICA HAVE
BEEN MOVING
APART
IGUANODON
122 MYA
121 MYA
MAMMALS
ARE
LYING LOW
EOMAIA
125
MILLION
YEARS AGO

COUNTDOWN TO THE DEATH OF THE DINOSAURS
Here's one for all you Mass Extinction Fans! And this time it's not just Earth's own climate causing chaos – there's an extra random factor . . .
. . . ALAN THE ASTEROID!
Alan is 10 kilometres wide, about the size of Mount Everest, and travelling at 100,000 km an hour.
66 MILLION
Here we are, 66 million years ago . . . and the Age of the Dinosaurs has been going on for a REALLY LONG TIME (in fact, for well over 100 million years).
107 MYA
MICRORAPTOR
CONFUCIUSORNIS
104
SOUTH AMERICA AND AFRICA ARE BREAKING APART . . .
100 MILLION YEARS AGO
. . . MAKING THE ATLANTIC OCEAN
BEE
FIRST FLOWERING PLANTS
97
MYA
95
MYA
SPINOSAURUS
90
MYA
89
MYA
MOSASAUR
IT'S A WARM GREENHOUSE WORLD
87
MYA
86
MYA
ANKYLOSAURUS

YEARS
AGO
These dinosaurs have simply NO IDEA that a mega-asteroid is just about to cause the wiping-out of ALL the dinosaurs.*
*Well, not quite all the dinosaurs. Some got through, and nowadays we call them **birds**.
COUNTDOWN TO THE DEATH OF THE DINOSAURS
Alan approaches Earth and slams down in the Gulf of Mexico.
Alan ploughs 40km through the crust and into the mantle, leaving a crater over 160km wide.
There's a huge shockwave and firestorm, a global ash cloud and rain of hot rock. Everything burns. Earth is on fire. There's darkness and winter; plants die, causing a cascade of animal death. Good grief it's bad.
The dust settles.
10 thousand years pass and creatures start to come out, blinking in the daylight.
They've been underground.
And a lot of them are **MAMMALS**.
PARASAUROLOPHUS
VELOCIRAPTOR
PTERANODON
ANT
77 MYA
76 MYA
TRICERATOPS
VAST LAVA FLOWS AT THE DECCAN TRAPS
TYRANNOSAURUS
HERE COMES ALAN THE ASTEROID
WHAM!
66 MILLION YEARS AGO
64 MYA
MASS EXTINCTION
61 MYA

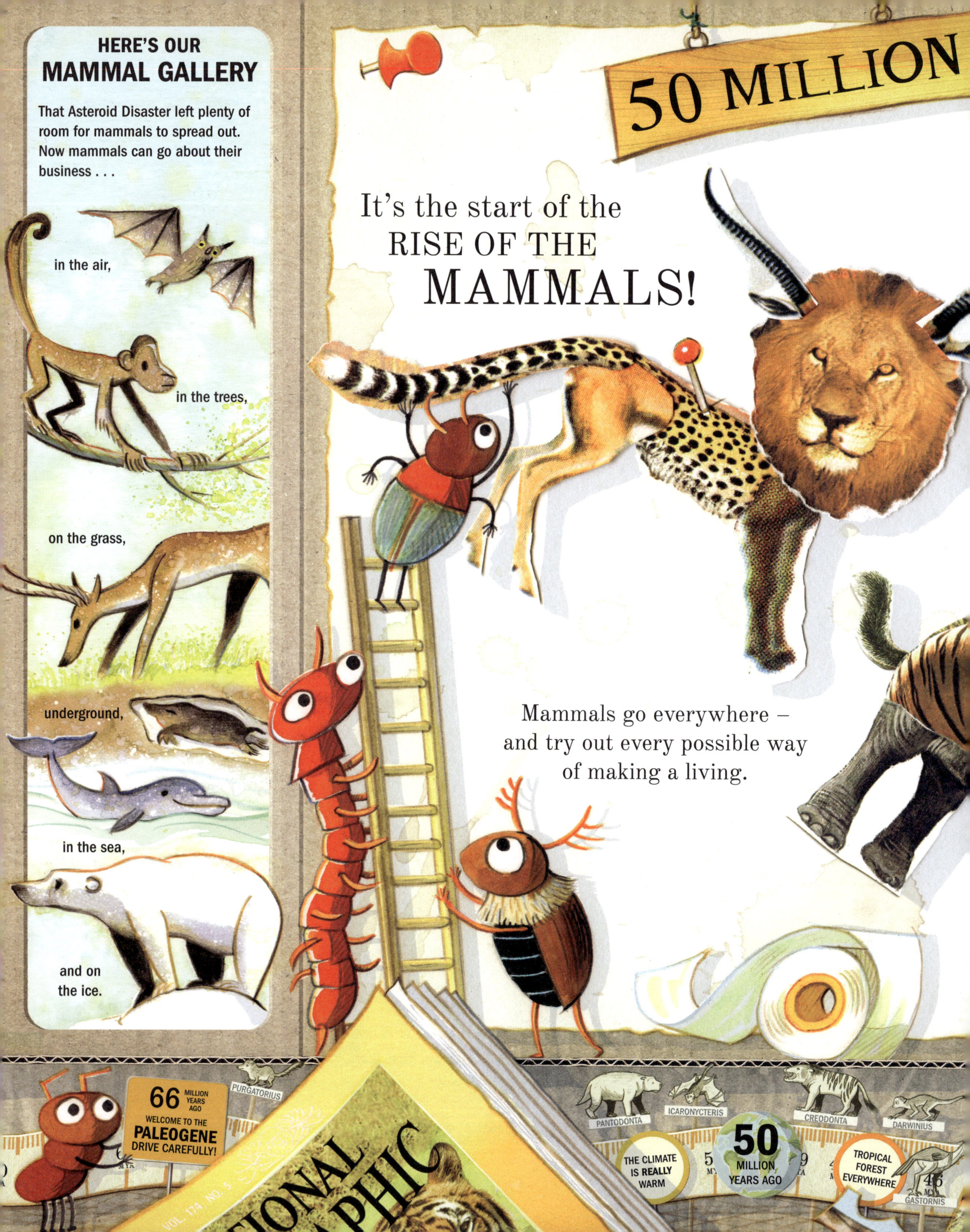
HERE'S OUR
MAMMAL GALLERY
That Asteroid Disaster left plenty of room for mammals to spread out. Now mammals can go about their business . . .
in the air,
in the trees,
on the grass,
underground,
in the sea,
and on the ice.
50 MILLION
It's the start of the RISE OF THE MAMMALS!
Mammals go everywhere – and try out every possible way of making a living.
66 MILLION YEARS AGO
WELCOME TO THE PALEOGENE
DRIVE CAREFULLY!
PURGATORIUS
VOL. 174, NO. 5
PANTODONTA
ICARONYCTERIS
CREODONTA
DARWINIUS
THE CLIMATE IS REALLY WARM
50 MILLION YEARS AGO
TROPICAL FOREST EVERYWHERE
GASTORNIS

YEARS AGO
BACK WHALE
70 ft.
We've made some mammals here from parts we cut out of a magazine.
Prott
SO WHAT'S SO GOOD ABOUT BEING A MAMMAL?
FUR
Mmmmm, everyone likes fur.
Lots of different types of
TEETH
for grinding and chewing and nibbling and ripping and gnawing.
Feeding your babies
MILK
Generating your own
CENTRAL HEATING
so that you can keep active, even when it's cold.
This means you can live almost
ANYWHERE.
BASILOSAURUS
PARICTIS
GRASSLANDS APPEAR
MESOHIPPUS
PALAEOLAGUS
LEPTOMERYX
ARSINOITHERIUM
BAD DRIVING! INDIA IS CRASHING INTO ASIA . . .
. . . PUSHING UP THE HIMALAYAS
36 MYA
35 MYA
30 MYA
26 MYA
24 MYA
22 MYA
21 MYA

HERE WE ARE ON THE ICE-AGE PLAINS
2 MILLION YEARS AGO.

It's cold and dry, and around here no trees, just lots of grass.

To survive, you need to be keen on eating grass. (Or keen on eating the ones who like eating grass.) Being big and furry is a good idea, too.

BEAR DOG

ENALIARCTOS

23 MILLION YEARS AGO
YOU HAVE REACHED
THE NEOGENE

20 MILLION YEARS AGO

CHALICOTHERIUM

AEPYCAMELUS

DEINOTHERIUM

EARTH'S CLIMATE IS MILD . . .

. . . WITH LOTS OF GRASSLANDS

ICEHOUSE
EARTH IS IN COOLING MODE
(It was those Himalayas. CO_2 levels dropped.)

31 MYA · 30 MYA · 29 MYA · 28 MYA · 27 MYA · 26 MYA · 25 MYA · 24 MYA · 23 MYA · 22 MYA · 15 MYA

years ago
It's the
AGE OF ICE.
Earth gets thrown
in the Deep Freeze
again and again.
FROM GREENHOUSE
TO ICEHOUSE
For most of its life, the Earth has been a GREENHOUSE planet, with NO ICE at the North or South poles. The sea level is so high that lots of the edges of the continents are under water, creating warm, shallow seas.
GREENHOUSE
EARTH
But when the Earth flips into an ICEHOUSE planet, white ice keeps the poles cold. The sea level is lower, so all that underwater continent becomes lots of dry land.
ICEHOUSE
EARTH
The planet has pulsed between an icy world and an unfrozen one for millions of years, and we're at the end of an ice age right now.
GLYPTODON
2.5 MILLION YEARS AGO
THE CYCLE OF THE ICE AGE BEGINS
NOW
Let's have a closer look at that last million years . . .

SO WHAT'S SO GOOD ABOUT BEING A

HUMAN?

Have a look at this very odd animal.

We have . . .

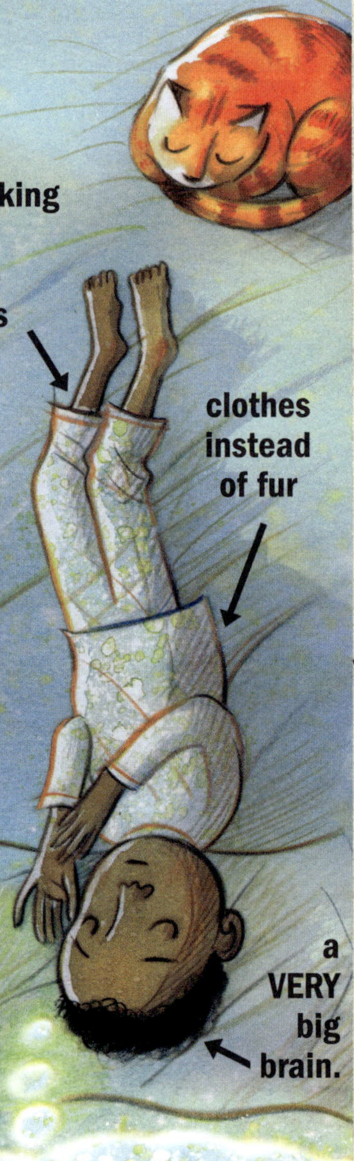

walking on two legs

clothes instead of fur

a VERY big brain.

And maybe the most mighty superpower of all: **IMAGINATION.**

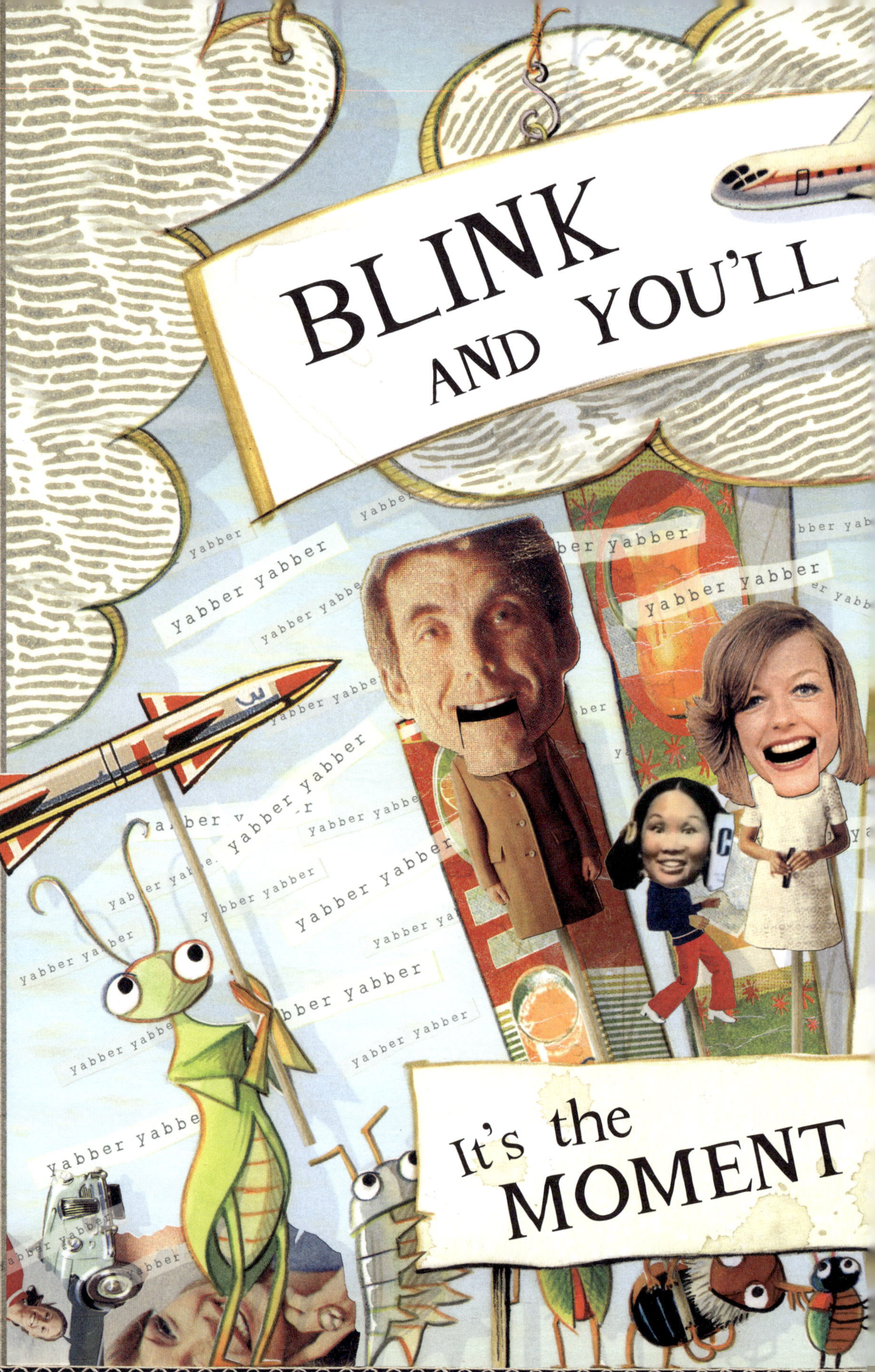

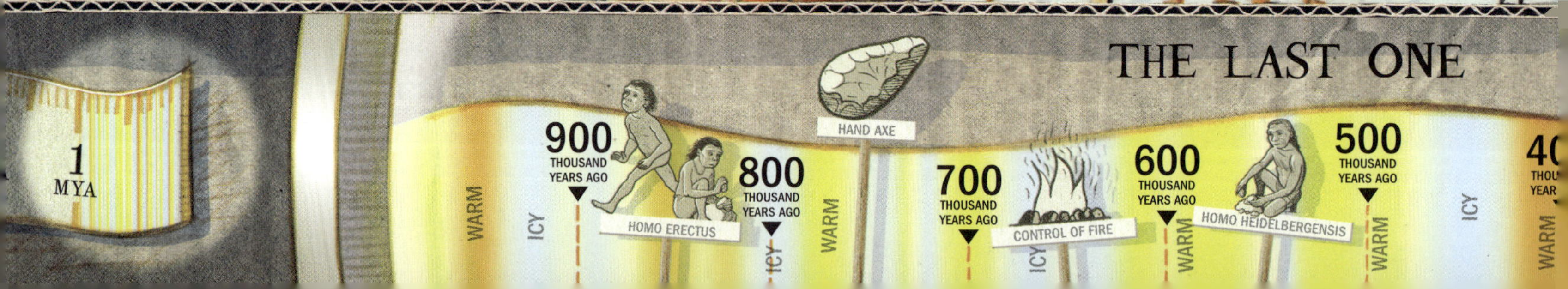

BLINK AND YOU'LL

It's the MOMENT

THE LAST ONE

900 THOUSAND YEARS AGO

WARM

ICY

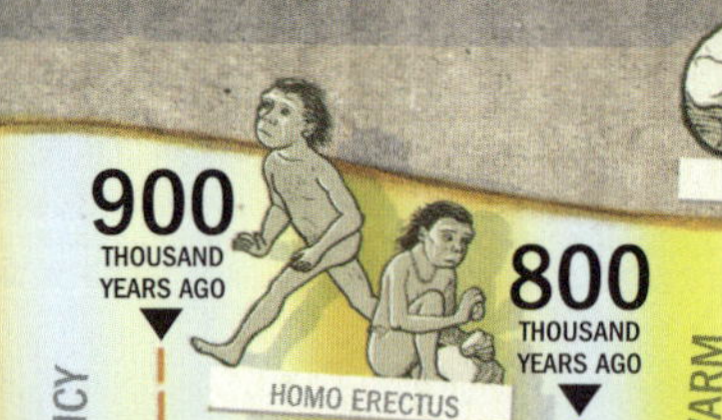

800 THOUSAND YEARS AGO

ICY

WARM

700 THOUSAND YEARS AGO

ICY

600 THOUSAND YEARS AGO

WARM

500 THOUSAND YEARS AGO

WARM

ICY

WARM

40[0] THOU[SAND] YEAR[S AGO]

SO WHAT'S SO GOOD ABOUT BEING A HUMAN?

With their hyperactive imaginations, humans really have been busy. Here are just a few human inventions:

COOKING FOOD
SPEARS
CLOTHES
GUNS
THE ALPHABET
BOOKS
THE PAST AND THE FUTURE
CHAIRS
THE PIANO
LEMON MERINGUE PIE
SCIENCE
ZERO
PAPER
MAPS
PHOTOGRAPHS
PLASTIC
FARMING

Humans have reshaped and refilled the Earth.

BIOMASS OF ALL MAMMALS: HUMAN ERA YEAR 2020

MILLION YEARS

I'm feeling dizzy,
my head is swimming . . .
in fact, I AM
swimming . . .
in some sort of
animal soup
of life!
ORIGIN OF SPECI
endless forms most
beautiful and most wonderful
have been, and are being, evolved.
It's the LAST MILLIMETRE on the Tape Measure of Time . . .
THIS MUCH!
THE LAST HUNDRED THOUSAND
90 THOUSAND YEARS AGO
EARTH'S CLIMATE IS COOLING
80 THOUSAND YEARS AGO
THE ERUPTION OF MOUNT TOBA MAKES 6 YEARS OF WINTER
70 THOUSAND YEARS AGO
MASTODON
60
DEINOTHERIUM
CASTOROIDES
50 THOUSAND YEARS AGO
MEGATHERIUM

Err, Rod . . . ? We were wondering – are we finished now?
YEARS
DEEP FREEZE
ICE ON EARTH IS AT A MAXIMUM
MAMMOTH
MEGALOCEROS
DIRE WOLF
MEGAFAUNA START MYSTERIOUSLY DISAPPEARING
11,700 YEARS AGO
WELCOME TO THE HOLOCENE
ENJOY THE WARM AND FRIENDLY CLIMATE
10 THOUSAND YEARS AGO
PEOPLE BEGIN FARMING
DOMESTIC CAT
5
DOMESTIC DOG
1 THOUSAND YEARS AGO
CHICKEN
INVENTION OF THE STEAM ENGINE
LOTS OF CO_2 FROM PEOPLE BURNING FOSSIL FUELS . . .
. . . IS MAKING EARTH HEAT UP
Here's an **EVEN CLOSER LOOK** at the last hundred thousand years on the Tape Measure of Time.

IN 1 BILLION YEARS

IN 4 BILLION YEARS

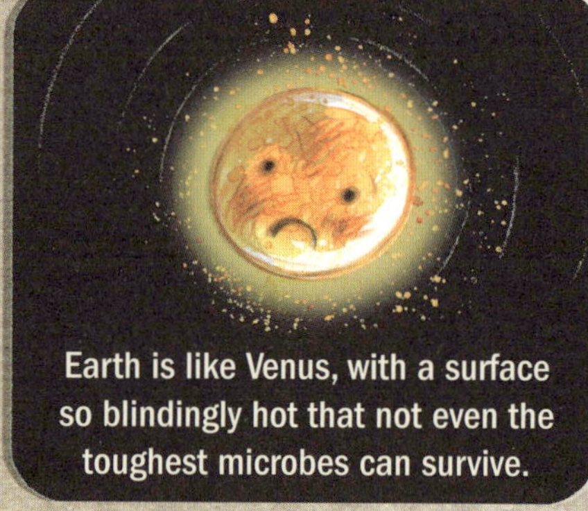

IN 8 BILLION YEARS

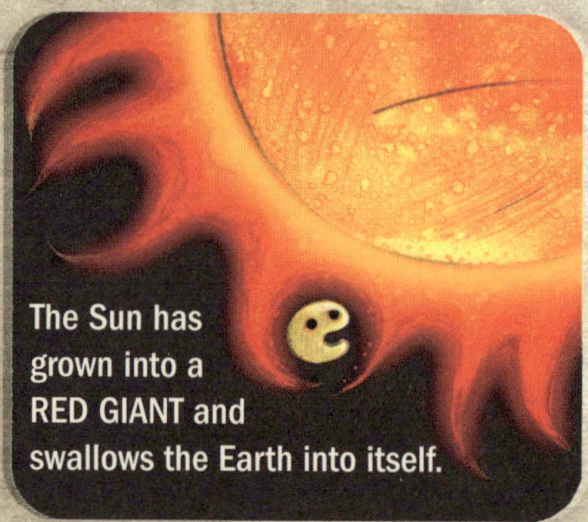

WE ARE ALL STARDUST.

What

Well, we've reached the end of the Encyclopedia now, and that just about wraps it up for the

Greatest Show on Earth.

Actually, the Earth is **ONLY HALFWAY** through its life, and there are still **500 MILLION** more years of animal life to come.

Next?
And quite a lot can happen in 500 million years.
It just did, after all.
So let's have a gaze into the future and see what's in store for Planet Earth.
Souvenir of Earth
VESUVIUS MATCHES
MEANWHILE, BACK IN
THE NEARER FUTURE
There are still 500 MILLION YEARS for animal life of all kinds.
Who knows WHAT could happen:
Space Rodents,
Snake Overlords,
Insect Overlords,
Fungus Overlords . . .
OR EVEN, YOU NEVER KNOW . . .
. . . Future Humans who can live in balance with everybody else.

OLD BOILER
MATCHES
PARTY
BOVIS
BEST BEFORE
46
PRIMORDIAL

That's all, folks!
So, as we close the curtain, let's give a
BIG ROUND OF APPLAUSE
to the Troupe.
It's the end of the show – but the
story of Life on Earth will go on!
NATIONAL GEOGRAPHIC

Welcome to the

. . . where you can find definitions for some of the words we used.

Amphibian A (usually) four-legged animal that spends at least part of its life in water, where it lays its eggs.

Arthropods Animals that have a hard outside covering called an exoskeleton. Insects, scorpions, crabs and spiders are all arthropods.

Asteroids Rocky objects, much smaller than planets, that orbit the Sun.

Atmosphere The layer of gases that surrounds Earth and contain the air we breathe. Nowadays it is made mostly of nitrogen and oxygen.

Blue-Green Algae A type of microbe that makes its food by using the sun's energy and carbon dioxide from the air, releasing oxygen. Also known as cyanobacteria.

Carbon This important element is found in all living things, and combines with other elements very easily. Diamonds, coal and graphite are forms of carbon.

Carbon dioxide or **CO_2** A gas that is present in small amounts in the air. Plants need it in order to breathe. It is one of the greenhouse gases, which trap heat from the Sun and make the planet warmer.

Climate The average weather for somewhere over a long period of time described by measurements of things like temperature, rainfall and sunshine.

Condense This is when a gas turns into a liquid. When warm steam in the air meets a cold surface it condenses, turning back into water.

Continent The continents are the huge land masses on Earth that are separated by the waters of the oceans.

Deccan Traps This is a huge area in India where volcanic activity made vast outpourings of lava around 66 million years ago.

Digit A finger, thumb or toe.

Element This is a substance made up of only one type of atom. Oxygen, carbon, iron and gold are all elements.

Encyclopedia A book containing information about EVERYTHING, in alphabetical order.

Evaporate This is when a liquid gets enough energy to turn into a gas, for example, hot water turning into steam.

Excretion How a body passes out waste stuff it doesn't need. Usually out of a special hole.

Himalayas A huge mountain range in the north of India.

Ice Age This is a time when thick ice sheets called glaciers cover large areas of the Earth.

Lava Hot, liquid rock that flows from a volcano or other opening in the surface of the Earth. When the liquid rock is still underground it is called **magma**.

Limb An arm, leg or wing.

Magma This is **lava** that is still underground.

Magnetic field This is the area around a magnet that is affected by its magnetic force. The Earth's **magnetic field** is created by electric currents in the Earth's core.

Mammals Warm-blooded, usually furry animals that make milk to feed their young.

Mantle This is the thick layer of the Earth that lies between the crust and the core. The continents float on the **mantle** like massive icebergs.

Mass extinction This is when a large number of species of creatures over a vast area all die out in a short period of time.

Megafauna The largest animals existing (usually on land) in a particular time. Modern **megafauna** include elephants, giraffes and rhinos.

Microbes Tiny living things – so small that they can't be seen by people without a microscope. Yeast – the ingredient that makes bread rise – is an example of a microbe.

Molecule These form when two or more atoms (the basic building blocks for everything in the universe) join together to make new substances. Water molecules are formed of two hydrogen atoms and one oxygen atom (H_2O).

H

H

Orchestra pit This is the area in front of the stage at a theatre where the musicians usually play their instruments.

Oxygen An element that makes up 21% of the Earth's air and is essential for animal and plant life.

Photosynthesis This is where living things, especially plants, use energy from sunlight, combined with water, to turn carbon dioxide gas in the air into sugar that they eat to survive. The process produces oxygen, which is released into the air.

Plate tectonics The process that moves continental land masses round the Earth, powered by volcanic activity from inside the Earth.

Predator An animal that hunts other animals for food.

Red Giant A dying star that has expanded and cooled.

Reptiles A group of cold-blooded animals that have skin covered with small hard scales and lay eggs. Snakes, lizards and crocodiles are **reptiles**.

Rodents Mammals with long, sharp front teeth that they use for gnawing.

Shockwave A wave of energy that starts with an explosion or earthquake and moves through the air or ground with intense force.

Solar wind A stream of fast-travelling charged particles that pour out from the Sun and travel throughout the **solar system**. Earth's **magnetic field** shields us from the solar wind. Luckily.

Supercontinent A large area of land that has more than one continental core, or craton. They are formed by continental plates coming together.

Tetrapod An animal with four limbs (arms, legs or wings). Reptiles, amphibians, birds and mammals are all tetrapods.

THE TIME PERIODS OF THE EARTH

0.011 HOLOCENE

NEOGENE

23

PALEOGENE

66

CRETACEOUS

145

JURASSIC

201

TRIASSIC

252

PERMIAN

298

CARBONIFEROUS

358

DEVONIAN

419

SILURIAN

443

ORDOVICIAN

485

CAMBRIAN

541

EDIACARAN

THE PRECAMBRIAN

MILLION YEARS AGO

To Herbie

(and to the Natural History Museum, Oxford, where this all started)

– M.G.

With special thanks to Professor Paul Smith and Professor David Waltham for their very generous help.

PUFFIN BOOKS
UK | USA | Canada | Ireland | Australia | India | New Zealand | South Africa
Puffin Books is part of the Penguin Random House group of companies whose addresses can be found at global.penguinrandomhouse.com.
First published in hardback 2022
First published in paperback 2023

A CIP catalogue record for this book is available from the British Library
ISBN: 978-0-241-48085-4 Printed in China 004
The authorized representative in the EEA is Penguin Random House Ireland, Morrison Chambers, 32 Nassau Street, Dublin D02 YH68